STEM

SUPERSTAR
WOMEN

JOCELYN
BELL BURNELL

Discovering Pulsars

Megan Borgert-Spaniol

Checkerboard
Library

An Imprint of Abdo Publishing
abdopublishing.com

abdopublishing.com

Published by Abdo Publishing, a division of ABDO, PO Box 398166, Minneapolis, Minnesota 55439. Copyright © 2018 by Abdo Consulting Group, Inc. International copyrights reserved in all countries. No part of this book may be reproduced in any form without written permission from the publisher. Checkerboard Library™ is a trademark and logo of Abdo Publishing.

Printed in the United States of America, North Mankato, Minnesota
102017
012018

THIS BOOK CONTAINS
RECYCLED MATERIALS

Design: Emily O'Malley, Mighty Media, Inc.
Production: Mighty Media, Inc.
Editor: Liz Salzmann
Cover Photograph: STFC
Interior Photographs: Alamy, pp. 9, 27; AP Images, p. 23; Daily Herald Archive/National Museum of Science & Media/Science & Society Picture Library, p. 13; Getty Images, p. 21; Jocelyn Bell Burnell, pp. 15, 28 (right); Jodrell Bank, University of Manchester/Wikimedia Commons, p. 11; NASA, p. 17; NASA (X-ray: NASA/CXC/SAO; Infrared: NASA/JPL-Caltech), p. 19; Shutterstock, pp. 7, 28 (left), 29 (right); STFC, pp. 5, 25, 29 (left)

Publisher's Cataloging-in-Publication Data
Names: Borgert-Spaniol, Megan, author.
Title: Jocelyn Bell Burnell: discovering pulsars / by Megan Borgert-Spaniol.
Other titles: Discovering pulsars
Description: Minneapolis, Minnesota : Abdo Publishing, 2018. | Series: STEM superstar women | Includes online resources and index.
Identifiers: LCCN 2017944044 | ISBN 9781532112782 (lib.bdg.) | ISBN 9781532150500 (ebook)
Subjects: LCSH: Burnell, Jocelyn Bell, 1943-.--Juvenile literature. | Women physicists--Juvenile literature. | Northern Ireland--Juvenile literature.
Classification: DDC 530.092 [B]--dc23
LC record available at https://lccn.loc.gov/2017944044

CONTENTS

//

1

JOCELYN BELL BURNELL

Jocelyn Bell Burnell is a British **astrophysicist**. She made a major scientific discovery when she was only 24 years old. She went on to do important astronomic research. Burnell also became a highly respected teacher and professor.

Burnell's success has not been without disappointment. In many ways, her career was affected by the expectations for women of her time. Many people did not take her commitment to her career seriously. As a wife and mother, she could not always give her work top **priority**. Today, Burnell is a strong supporter of women in science.

> **"Scientists should never claim that something is absolutely true. You should never claim perfect, or total, or 100 percent, because you never, ever get there."**
>
> –Jocelyn Bell Burnell

Burnell spoke at the 8th Appleton Space Conference in December 2012. It was held at the Rutherford Appleton Laboratory in Oxfordshire, England.

From a young age, Burnell's parents encouraged her to ask questions and find answers. She developed a love for unexpected results in the search for new knowledge. For Burnell, the surprises are what make science exciting.

EDUCATION ENCOURAGED

Susan Jocelyn Bell was born on July 15, 1943, in Belfast, Northern Ireland. She went by her middle name, Jocelyn. Jocelyn grew up in a large farmhouse near Belfast with her parents and three younger **siblings**.

Education was important in Jocelyn's family. Her father, George Philip Bell, was an **architect**. He loved to learn about all kinds of topics. George encouraged Jocelyn to explore the books he brought home from the library. He also taught his children how to reason and ask questions.

FAITH AND SCIENCE

Jocelyn was raised as a Quaker. Quakers are members of the religious group the Society of Friends. Quakers believe each person experiences God in his or her own way. Their services are simpler than those of most other religions. She is still an active member today. In 2013, she published a lecture on being a scientist with religious beliefs.

Jocelyn's mother was Margaret Allison Bell. She didn't get to go to college. Margaret's family didn't have much money. They decided to send Margaret's younger brother to school and not her. At that time, people thought it was more important to educate boys than girls.

Belfast is about an hour's drive from Jocelyn's childhood home. Belfast is the capital of Northern Ireland.

3
A TALENT FOR PHYSICS

Margaret did not want her daughters to miss out on a good education. Jocelyn attended a local school with her younger sisters and brother. At the age of 11, she took an important test. The test was to determine whether she should continue her **academic** studies to prepare for college. Students who failed the test took classes to learn a trade, instead of preparing for college. Jocelyn failed the test.

However, Jocelyn's parents knew she could succeed academically. They convinced the school to keep Jocelyn in the academic classes. During the following two years, Jocelyn studied astronomy, **physics**, and other sciences. She received top scores on her tests.

Jocelyn's parents could see that she had a talent for science. They brought home books so she could learn on her own. When Jocelyn was 13 years old, she went away to **boarding school** in York, England.

Jocelyn's boarding school was the Mount School. Only girls went there.

Jocelyn stood out as a **physics** student at **boarding school**. Most of her classmates struggled with the subject. They often went to Jocelyn for help. Jocelyn spent many evenings explaining the homework to her peers. She discovered that she was good at and enjoyed teaching. Jocelyn's physics teacher also recognized her talent.

4

FUTURE IN THE STARS

Back home, Jocelyn's father was doing **architecture** work at the Armagh Observatory near Belfast. As a teenager, Jocelyn sometimes went with him to the observatory. The staff there showed Jocelyn the telescopes and encouraged her interest in the stars. After reading some of her father's astronomy books, Jocelyn fell in love with the subject.

Jocelyn knew she wanted to be an astronomer. But she was not sure if it was the field for her. Jocelyn did not like the idea of working at night, as most astronomers did. Then Jocelyn discovered **radio astronomy**. This was a subject she could study during the day. It was also a subject that used **physics**. Jocelyn decided she would be a radio astronomer.

DID YOU KNOW?

American **engineer** Karl Jansky first discovered radio signals from stars in 1932. A few years later, American astronomer Grote Reber built the first radio telescope.

The teachers at Jocelyn's school had never heard of **radio astronomy**. So, Jocelyn wrote a letter to Bernard Lovell. He was a well-known English radio astronomer at the time. Jocelyn asked him which subjects she should study to become a radio astronomer. Lovell wrote back. He told Jocelyn to continue studying **physics** at college.

Lovell built the Lovell Telescope at the Jodrell Bank Observatory in 1957. At the time, it was the largest radio telescope in the world. Today it is the third-largest.

5

GLASGOW TO CAMBRIDGE

In the early 1960s, Bell started college at the University of Glasgow in Scotland. There, she was the only female in her **physics** class of 50 students. Her male peers often teased her. They would stomp their feet and bang on their desks when she entered the class. But Bell wouldn't let her classmates discourage her. She knew she had to study physics to become an astronomer. She learned to ignore the taunts.

In 1965, Bell graduated with a physics degree from the University of Glasgow. Later that year, she moved to the

WHAT ARE QUASARS?

Quasar is short for "quasi-stellar radio source." These star-like objects are extremely bright. However, they do not appear bright from Earth. This is because they are found in distant space. Their light takes billions of years to reach Earth!

Bell at the Mullard Radio Astronomy Observatory in 1968

University of Cambridge in England. There, Bell started working toward her **PhD** in **radio astronomy**.

At Cambridge, Bell assisted in a research project led by radio astronomer Antony Hewish. They worked at the Mullard Radio Astronomy Observatory near the university. The purpose of the research project was to study quasars. These bright masses of energy deep in space give off **radio waves**. Bell's job was to help build a telescope to record these waves.

6

THE RADIO TELESCOPE

Bell worked with a team to build the radio telescope. They drove thousands of posts into the ground. They strung miles of wires and cables from the posts. After two years, they had built a giant radio telescope called the Interplanetary Scintillation Array. The telescope covered about four acres (1.6 ha). That is the size of more than 60 tennis courts!

In 1967, the telescope was ready to detect **radio waves** from deep space. Radio waves cannot be directly seen. So, the telescope recorded them as lines on paper.

HARD LABOR

Building the radio telescope required a lot of physical work. Bell built up her arm muscles driving posts into the ground. At the time, Bell played on a **field hockey** team. After working on the radio telescope, she could hit the ball farther than she ever had before. Her teammates could barely keep up!

Every day, the telescope printed out 96 feet (30 m) of paper. It was Bell's job to **analyze** the recorded **radio waves**. She spent most of her afternoons and evenings studying these printouts.

Bell with the radio telescope she helped build

7

STRANGE WAVES

Bell reviewed hundreds of feet of telescope recordings over many weeks. She was looking for patterns that represented quasars. When she found a quasar, she would measure its size and observe any changes in the quasar.

Then, in October 1967, she noticed a different pattern of **radio waves**. These waves came in pulses, or bursts of energy. The pulses came from a single point in the sky at the same time every night. Bell knew the pulses were not coming from quasars. But what were they coming from?

Bell showed Hewish what she had discovered. He had never seen such a pattern before. The research team continued to examine the radio pulses. They wondered if the pulses were signals from life forms outside the solar system. For a while, they nicknamed the pulses "little green men."

Then, Bell discovered a second set of pulses. These radio waves came from a different part of the sky.

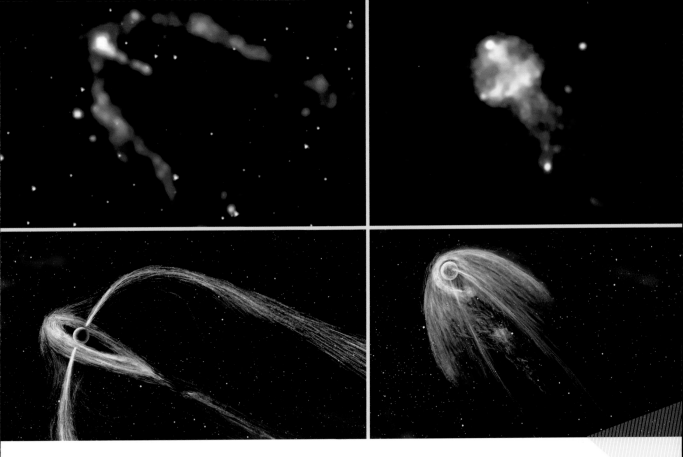

Instead of drawing lines on paper, today's telescopes use X-rays to take photos of pulsars (*top images*). But these images are often blurry. So, artists draw detailed illustrations of what astronomers believe the pulsars look like (*bottom images*).

Now Bell knew the signals were not coming from extraterrestrial beings. They were from a new kind of star-like object in space. Bell's team called them pulsating radio stars. They later came to be known as pulsars.

8

PULSARS AND NEUTRON STARS

This was a busy time for Bell. She still had to complete the quasars project to earn her **PhD**. But now she was also working with Hewish to learn more about pulsars. In February 1968, Bell and Hewish published a paper about their findings. News spread about their discovery of pulsars.

NEUTRON STARS

A neutron star is the small, **dense** core that remains after a large star explodes. Neutron stars are about ten miles (16 km) across, but they each weigh more than the sun! Neutron stars spin several times per second. They also have a very strong **magnetic field**. The field creates a beam of **radio waves**. The waves can be detected from Earth every time a neutron star rotates. Neutron stars detected from Earth are called pulsars.

Astronomers all over the world began their own pulsar research. Months later, British astronomer Thomas Gold presented an explanation for pulsars. He linked the pulsars to neutron stars. These **dense**, spinning stars give off **radio waves** that sweep through space. Bell's pulsar discovery proved the existence of neutron stars.

An image taken by NASA's Chandra X-ray Observatory in 2009 of a neutron star surrounded by a cloud of particles

9

GAMMA RAYS AND X-RAYS

Bell completed the work for her **PhD** in **radio astronomy** in 1968. That same year, she married Martin Burnell and changed her name to Jocelyn Bell Burnell. Martin worked for the British government. His job required him to move often. Burnell knew that by marrying him, she would have to move too.

The Burnells settled in southern England. There, Burnell began doing astronomy research at the University of Southampton. In 1970, she became a **physics** teacher at the university.

In 1973, Burnell gave birth to a son, Gavin. At this time, she stopped teaching. She worked as an editor for an astronomy magazine called *The Observatory*. She also

DID YOU KNOW?

British and American scientists worked together on Ariel V. The **satellite** was in orbit from 1974 to 1980.

Burnell in her office at Mullard Space Science Laboratory

tutored students through a school called Open University. Burnell worked from home while caring for Gavin.

By 1974, the Burnells had moved to London. There, Burnell worked at the Mullard Space Science Laboratory. Her job was to observe and **analyze** data for a **satellite** called Ariel V. The satellite tracked **X-ray** sources in outer space.

10

NOBEL PRIZE NEWS

October 15, 1974, was an important day in Burnell's life. The Ariel V **satellite** had launched that morning. And around midday, Burnell learned some exciting news. The 1974 **Nobel Prize** in **Physics** had been announced. It was being awarded to her Cambridge advisor, Antony Hewish, for the discovery of pulsars. He shared the award with another British astronomer, Martin Ryle.

Burnell was pleased. This was the first time the Nobel Prize in Physics had included astronomy. She considered this an important moment for her field. However, the

AWARDS AND HONORS

Although Burnell did not win the Nobel Prize, she received many other awards and honors over the years. In 1989, she was awarded the Herschel Medal for her contribution to **astrophysics**. She has also received honorary degrees from prominent universities including Harvard University in Massachusetts.

King Carl Gustaf of Sweden (*right*) presented the Nobel Prize to Hewish (*left*) at a ceremony in Stockholm, Sweden.

award had not acknowledged Burnell's role in discovering pulsars.

Burnell responded with grace. She noted that she had been a student at the time of the discovery. She said the prize had gone to the right people. However, many of Burnell's fellow scientists were upset. They believed she should have been included in the award.

11

PROFESSOR BELL BURNELL

///

In 1982, Burnell and her family moved to Scotland for her husband's job. Burnell found work at the Royal Observatory in Edinburgh. There, she was part of an international team working on a special telescope based in Hawaii. Burnell later became an officer at the Royal Observatory, where she worked for nearly ten years.

By 1991, Burnell was ready for another move. She and her husband had recently separated. Her son was in college. Burnell was free to go where she wanted. She found that Open University was looking for a **physics** professor. She applied for the job and was hired. She became the head of the physics department. During her ten years at Open University, Burnell achieved her mission to increase astronomy research in the department.

After Burnell left Open University, she served as Dean of Science at the University of Bath in England. She has also been a visiting professor at Princeton University

Burnell was part of a ceremony to officially open a LOFAR station in Chilbolton, England, in September 2010. LOFAR stands for Low-Frequency Array. The station has 96 radio telescope antennas to produce images of space.

in New Jersey and the University of Oxford in England. In 2014, she became president of the Royal Society of Edinburgh. The Royal Society is a charitable organization that promotes learning and research.

12

ASTROPHYSICS WHIZ

Burnell has become known for her extensive research in **astrophysics** and her teaching ability. She has helped many students understand difficult subjects, including **physics** and astronomy. Burnell is also known for the **barriers** she broke as a woman in science.

Today, Burnell often travels to schools and science events to give speeches and lectures. She talks to groups of girls and young women about her experiences. Burnell encourages these girls and women to take an interest in math and science.

STEM WOMEN

When Burnell became a professor at Open University, she was only the second female professor of physics in England. And she was the first female president of both the Royal Astronomical Society and the Institute of Physics. Today, Burnell is a spokesperson for women in STEM (science, **technology**, **engineering**, and mathematics).

But Burnell is most famous for her pulsar discovery. Her observation and **analysis** led to important advancements in astronomy. In 2015, The United Kingdom's Royal Society awarded Burnell the Royal Medal. This honor acknowledged Burnell's role in one of the most important astronomical discoveries of the twentieth century.

In 2007, Burnell was made a Dame Commander of the British Empire by Queen Elizabeth II of England. The award was for Burnell's contributions to science. She is now known as Dame Jocelyn Bell Burnell.

TIMELINE

///////////////////////////

1943

Susan Jocelyn Bell is born in Belfast, Northern Ireland, on July 15.

1965

Bell graduates from the University of Glasgow. She begins studying radio astronomy at the University of Cambridge.

1967

Bell discovers pulsating radio stars, later called "pulsars."

1968

Bell finishes the work for her PhD in radio astronomy. She marries Martin Burnell.

1974

Burnell researches X-ray astronomy at Mullard Space Science Laboratory in London. X-ray satellite Ariel V launches in October.

1982

Burnell moves to Scotland and begins research at the Royal Observatory.

1989

Burnell receives the Herschel Medal from the Royal Astronomical Society.

1991

Burnell is hired as professor and chair of the physics department at Open University in England.

2014

Burnell becomes president of the Royal Society of Edinburgh.

2015

Burnell receives the Royal Medal for her contributions in observing, analyzing, and understanding pulsars.

GLOSSARY

//////////////////////////////

academic—relating to school or education.

analyze—to examine something closely to learn the nature and relationship of its parts. An instance of analyzing is an analysis.

architecture—the art of planning and designing buildings. A person who designs architecture is called an architect.

astrophysics—a branch of astronomy. Astrophysics is the study of the behavior and measurements of objects outside Earth's atmosphere. A scientist who studies astrophysics is an astrophysicist.

barrier—something that blocks the way or makes something difficult.

boarding school—a school that students may live in during the year.

dense—having a high mass per unit volume.

engineering—the application of science and mathematics to design and create useful structures, products, or systems. A person who does this is an engineer.

field hockey—a game that is played on a field in which each team uses curved sticks to try to hit a ball into the opponent's goal.

magnetic field—the region around a magnetic object or an electric current in which the magnetic forces can be detected.

Nobel Prize—any of six annual awards given to people who have made the greatest contributions to humankind. The prizes are awarded for physics, chemistry, medicine, economics, literature, and peace.

PhD—doctor of philosophy. Usually, this is the highest degree a student can earn in a subject.

physics—a science that studies matter and energy and how they interact.

priority—the condition of coming before others, as in order or importance.

radio astronomy—a type of astronomy that studies radio waves from outer space. A scientist who studies radio astronomy is a radio astronomer.

radio wave—a type of electromagnetic wave. Natural radio waves are created by lightning or space objects. Artificial radio waves are used in communication and navigation systems.

satellite—a manufactured object that orbits Earth. It relays scientific information back to Earth.

sibling—a brother or a sister.

technology—the use of science in solving problems.

tutor—to teach a student privately.

X-ray—an invisible and powerful light wave that can pass through solid objects.

ONLINE RESOURCES

Booklinks
NONFICTION NETWORK
FREE! ONLINE NONFICTION RESOURCES

To learn more about Jocelyn Bell Burnell, visit **abdobooklinks.com**. These links are routinely monitored and updated to provide the most current information available.

INDEX